MEDITERRANEAN DIET COOKBOOK 2022

RECIPES AND HEALTHY:
EASY MEDITERRANEAN RECIPES
EXPLAINED:
FOOD DIET RECIPES FOR BEGINNERS

SARA JACKLINE

Mediterranean Diet Cookbook 2022: Recipes And Healthy:

Easy Mediterranean Recipes Explained: Food Diet Recipes For Beginners

The Best Complete Mediterranean Diet

The Mediterranean consuming habitual is the call that has been given to a selected nutritional habitual that turned into to start with used by people in much less lucky districts of Italy and Greece for an extended time. This consuming habitual turned into now no longer to start with idea to be mainly strong in those areas, as people ate those nourishments because of need, in place of because of the Mediterranean weight-reduction plan weight loss and outstanding sustenance blessings they encountered. This kind of cooking is a ways now no longer pretty similar to what you will expect from this area, but it's far through and huge plenty greater superb due to the fact that such things as grease and unfold are now and again utilized.

What It Entails

Fundamentally, a Mediterranean weight-reduction plan requires people to devour plenty of latest herbal products, plant nourishments, fish, poultry, a few dairy objects at the same time as utilising extra virgin olive oil because the vital wellspring of fats. Additionally, a mild degree of eggs may be eaten each month, at the same time as pork is to live farfar from but a great deal as may want to fairly be expected. Red meat may be eaten in low sums, but suppers ought now no longer to be revolved round it attributable to the way it impacts the coronary heart. The Mediterranean weight-reduction plan is meant to deliver down the threat of coronary infection on account that olive oil is excessive in monounsaturated fat, that have been recognised to decrease this threat generously. This likewise decreases the frame's ldl cholesterol stages, that is moreover some thing fine for the frame.

History of the Mediterranean Diet

Despite the reality that this weight-reduction plan turned into first uncovered in 1945, it did not commonly hit general stages till the 1990s, while people commenced to accumulate a lately located interest to what they have been consuming. This is across the time that pastime suggests commenced displaying up on TV and proper weight-reduction plan commenced to end up well-known as soon as greater. The Mediterranean weight-reduction plan relies upon at the opportunity that people in those locales have a far slower tempo of coronary infection than people with comparative fats admission in specific areas of the world. For instance, an man or woman residing withinside the United States and an man or woman residing in Greece may want to consume exactly the identical degree of fats a reputedly countless quantity of time after a year, but the American could have a better opportunity of experiencing coronary infection because the man or woman in query is feeling the lack of unique additives from their weight-reduction plan.

Impacts on Health

The essential solving in a Mediterranean weight-reduction plan this is universal to have the maximum impact on an man or woman's well being is extra virgin olive oil. This is due to the fact that the weight-reduction plan is innately low in soaked fats, but the olive oil makes it excessive in monounsaturated fats, which (as lately referenced) is beneficial to your coronary heart. The Mediterranean weight-reduction plan is also excessive in nutritional fiber, which advances consistency of the belly associated framework. The weight-reduction plan can a number of the time be excessive in salt, while is contains:

Olives

Escapades

Serving of blended vegetables dressing

Fish roe

This salt substance is not in reality some thing poor in any case, in mild of the reality that the ones matters comprise not unusualplace salts the frame can make use of and ingest all of the greater serenely.

Exercise

One issue that severa people likely may not apprehend approximately Mediterranean weight-reduction plan weight loss is that the folks that commenced the consuming habitual for the maximum element labored outdoor and fairly hard. This implies they have been getting a whole lot of pastime each unmarried day, however outdoor air. This, withinside the blend with the little bits those humans could devour, precipitated pretty slim and sturdy bodies. This helped coronary heart power obviously, that is some other motivation in the back of why they skilled a ways fewer passings cardiovascular issues.

Clinical Findings

Various scientific investigations were directed at the Mediterranean weight-reduction plan and that they have located that guys who lived in Crete, that is one of the districts wherein this consuming habitual turned into to start with utilized, had a low prevalence of coronary infection. This passed off irrespective of the fact they in reality gobbled excessive measures of fat as a rule. One of the most important causes in the back of this locating is that massive numbers of those guys modified from margarine to extra virgin olive oil because it turned into greater affordable. They moreover had a excessive nutrient C admission and reduced the degree of pork contrasted with specific portions of the globe. It need to be observed that the discoveries of this research have been emotional to such an quantity that the results have been dispensed earlier than the exam were finished. This turned into due to the fact that the folks that have been main the exam did not in reality be given that they might continue to be quiet approximately the statistics anymore. Different diseases and illnesses that have been emphatically prompted through this weight-reduction plan comprise osteoporosis, proscribing the threat of sure styles of malignancy, sensitivities, Alzheimers infection and there are greater examinations being tried as I compose this article.

Weight reduction

Further examinations have indicated occurrences of Mediterranean weight-reduction plan weight loss, as 322 people partook in an ordeal wherein some humans have been based upon a low-carb diet, others embraced a low-fats consuming habitual, and a few ate only a Mediterranean weight-reduction plan. The results verified that the folks that have been at the Mediterranean consuming habitual had the pleasant weight loss of all, with the primary individuals dropping 12 and 10 kilos separately. The exam featured that the Mediterranean consuming habitual weight loss is robust and need to be taken into consideration through any man or woman who's experiencing issue getting greater fit.

Why Choose the Mediterranean Lifestyle

The Mediterranean consuming habitual is not most effective an method to get greater fit, but, is an method to absolutely remodel you, and in doing as such, supporting with drawing out it. The clinical benefits are unending, specially while they're joined with paintings out, making this nourishment enjoy some thing easily really well worth investigating. The principal subject is - the folks that are in this weight-reduction plan have decrease dying fees than the folks that are now no longer, that is motive sufficient to test it out.

On the off risk which you have a beyond packed with coronary infection on your family, you definitely cannot stand to continue with a comparable manner and now you've got got some other option.

Mediterranean Diet 2022

We realise that a Mediterranean food regimen have to be sound - we have got all determined the ones ads wherein greater set up people are frolicking approximately in olive forests like younger sheep next to appreciating a supper of olive oil and veggies. Furthermore, we moreover realise how delicious a Mediterranean ingesting recurring may be, with all of the faultless new flavors that invoke event recollections. Only one sniff of recent spices can circulate us lower back to a radiant Greek island...

The "Mediterranean Diet" may be streamlined into 3 components:

loads of olive oil, natural product, veggies, fish, oats, and veggies (peas, beans, and lentils)

slight quantities of wine - usually with meals

confined portions of meat, milk, and dairy items

Examination of the nutritional styles of 74,000 Europeans greater than 60 years of age exposed that a Mediterranean-kind eating regimen should suggest dwelling longer - via way of means of as lots as one yr.

While the maximum wonderful food regimen is low in soaked creature fat but excessive in unsaturated fat, in Britain we're devouring fewer meals grown from the floor and all of the greater full-fats dairy items, liquor, and soda pop - as indicated via way of means of the Office for National Statistics.

Further exam into the daily diets of Greek people has been allotted withinside the British Medical Journal and become accounted for withinside the Daily Telegraph paper in July 2008. In extra of 26,000 human beings had been checked for a totally long term and the results had been astounding. For the ones whose eating regimen took after the Mediterranean perfect intently, girls reduced their hazard of constructing up a huge variety of malignant increase via way of means of 16% and guys dwindled theirs via way of means of 9%.

In 2007 it become likewise assured that a Mediterranean ingesting recurring should help with forestalling the development of asthma, breathing hypersensitivities, and Alzheimer's Disease.

Another ongoing exam, allotted in The New England Journal of Medicine in

July 2008, notion approximately the influences of 3 well-known weight manipulate plans for greater than 2 years. Overweight people matured 44-59, dwelling in Israel, had been doled out indiscriminately to comply with both a low-fats ingesting recurring or a Mediterranean food regimen, or a low-sugar eating regimen.

In the low-fats food regimen gathering, eighty guys and 14 girls completed the exam and misplaced 3.4kg and 0.1kg separately.

This ingesting recurring trusted American Heart Association rules:

an power admission of 1800 kcal each day for guys and 1500 kcal for girls, with 30% of energy from fats, 10% of energy from immersed fats, and 300mg of ldl cholesterol each day.

In the Mediterranean ingesting recurring gathering, seventy six guys and 17 girls completed the research and misplaced 4.0kg and 6.2kg individually. This food regimen become excessive in veggies and occasional in purple meat, with chicken and fish supplanting hamburger and sheep; delivered fatwas from 30-45g olive oil and 5-7 nuts daily. Energy admission become 1800 kcal each day for guys and 1500 kcal for girls, with an goal of near 35% of energy from fats.

In the low-sugar eating regimen gathering, seventy seven guys and eight girls completed the exam and misplaced 4.9kg and 2.4kg individually. This ingesting recurring trusted the Atkins eating regimen and supposed to present 20g of sugars each day for the preliminary 2 months, increasing little by little to 120g each day. Admission of whole energy, protein, and fats become now no longer restricted, in spite of the truth that individuals had been knowledgeable to select out veggie lover reassets regarding fats and protein and to prevent hydrogenated/trans fat.

All gatherings shed kilos, with the finest misfortune charge occurring at some stage in the preliminary a 1/2 of yr.

While the guys might in widespread lose greater weight on a low-sugar eating regimen, the girls misplaced greater via way of means of following a Mediterranean ingesting recurring.

Be that because it may, the ones at the low-fats food regimen had recovered as much as 33% in their 1/2 of-yr weight loss following yr and a 1/2 of, earlier than their weight arrived at a steady state. The Atkins fitness meals nuts had a similar encounter, improving as much as a fourth in their 5-month weight loss following 15 months, previous to arriving at a level. Paradoxically, the collection following a Mediterranean ingesting recurring shed kilos speedy for a 1/2 of yr but stored on moving into form for a similarly a 1/2 of yr whilst their weight arrived at a steady worth, AND they failed to get better weight.

Mediterranean Recipes Diet Explained

The Mediterranean plan's food regimen is one which has been adjusted from the nourishments and plans discovered withinside the sixteen international locations flanking the Mediterranean Sea. Numerous nowadays bear in mind Mediterranean meals equal to Greek meals. Albeit Greek meals is lots of the equal, the alternative flanking international locations have had a massive effect also. Cooking strategies outgrew a rustic manner of lifestyles in which the greens, spices, and exclusive fixings are privately evolved with the aid of using little ranchers. Numerous spices and vegetables which are an outfit withinside the wild are moreover utilized.

Olive and lemon timber that are enormous portions of Mediterranean cooking fill properly withinside the locale. Local humans make use of severa spices constantly, for example, garlic, oregano, mint, thyme, and basil of their planning. Nourishments are saved as new as will be anticipated below the instances and people which are cooked can be cooked regularly with the hottest of fixings giving flavors time to merge.

Red meat is eaten typically near as soon as each month. Since the population is so close to the ocean, fish is a spine withinside the consuming regimen. Fish along certainly created cheeses, oils, natural merchandise, nuts, grains, greens, and greens are the basis in their consuming routine. Water in massive quantities is moreover gobbled robotically and crimson wine is burned-via with a few restraint. Desserts are normally gobbled as herbal merchandise which are decrease in energy and lots better in fiber and dietary supplements than candy cakes.

Due to the excessive usage of greens and greens and essentially no soaked fat, coronary contamination is located extensively much less often than withinside the US or exclusive international locations whose diets are excessive in crimson meats and dairy.

The New York Times and U.S. News and World Report each investigated introductory examinations displaying a ability lower in Alzheimer's contamination in people following this type of food regimen.

Despite the truth that I am now no longer a defender of "counts energy" essentially, the Mediterranean Diet is actually a very good weight-reduction plan plan using the hottest of fixings, no soaked fat, almost no crimson meat, and minimum subtle sugar.

How would possibly you be capable of doubtlessly now no longer shed kilos using this type of "consuming plan." what is more, the plans are easy and mostly take below 20 mins to get ready.

Food Recipes For Beginners - Raw Food Best Kept Secrets

The crude meals food plan has been polished for decades through the ones those who perceived the getting better and stimulating homes of crude meals. Crude nourishments allude to the ones nourishments that are herbal, all characteristic, and now no longer cooked over 118 degrees. This consists of herbal products, vegetables, seeds, nuts, vegetables, and an collection of ocean plants. These nourishments are very excessive in dietary supplements and fundamental vitamins and minerals making them excellent power promoters and mending specialists.

The consuming ordinary has numerous blessings at the frame beyond those empowering homes. They were regarded to assist in assimilations as they assist the frame unfastened itself of toxins and synthetics which have been accumulated over the lengthy haul.

These normal purifying aides detox your frame and may stop or maybe help put off infection and different frame sicknesses. People rehearsing the consuming ordinary have mentioned extra clean pores and skin, taken out "fluffiness" from the brain, a spike in power levels, even emotional weight loss. More awesome instances have even specific intense getting better, for example, the disposal of hypersensitivities, muscle torments, and at instances, in any occasion, relieving Diabetes.

The weight-reduction plan has severa blessings, anyway, severa human beings dread the consuming ordinary as they see it as tough and tedious. This is a normal inaccurate judgment.

Actually, it isn't any extra tough than a few different ordinary lifestyles change, and a "with none weaning period" method should not be used for it to be powerful. To get each one in every of its blessings, one clearly simply necessities to consume a more a part of crude meals of their weight-reduction plan. In the occasion that your weight-reduction plan incorporates commonly of 55-65% crude meals, at that factor you'll at gift choose up from the mending and stimulating blessings they preserve. These nourishments are likewise amazingly adaptable. You can at gift re-make a massive quantity of your gift maximum cherished dishes and make sandwiches, servings of blended greens, smoothies, pizzas, pies, and candy treats.

The maximum truthful method to consolidate a more quantity of those nourishments into your weight-reduction plan is thru crude meals plans for amateurs. These plans are whatever however hard to make, do not want high priced kitchen hardware, and make use of fundamental fixings discovered for your community merchant. It is a component of those crude meals plans for apprentices that preserve the hints of the trade. That is in view that you could make excellent getting better suppers that rush to plan.

For example one of the maximum truthful crude meals plans for amateurs is the morning meal smoothie. This smoothie joins greens, natural products, and spirulina, an ocean vegetable that allows the frame to ingest a couple of instances extra protein from it than from meat. These smoothies are pressed with power, and imperative dietary supplements to assist unfastened your organization of infection, artificial compounds, and poisons.

This consuming ordinary has been applied for pretty a long term to fix the frame and deliver power and weight loss options to human beings hoping to hold on with a stable manner of lifestyles. It has been regarded to have awesome results for human beings, all matters considered, and foundations. You can advantage admittance to a few first rate guidelines and mysteries of the crude meals food plan via crude meals plans for apprentices.

I am a functioning post-graduate who's passionate about wellbeing, meals, and utilising each to preserve a functioning manner of lifestyles. I am a veggie lover who has moreover rehearsed the vegetarian and crude meals food plan for massive timeframes.

I even have located them each very gainful for purchasing thinner, clearing pores and skin rashes, simply as mending one-of-a-kind portions of the frame. I am passionate about meals and love utilising my veggie lover/vegetarian/crude meals records to make awesome dishes and supper plans for human beings trying to likewise make each 2d count.

Easy Recipes - Perfect Work In The Kitchen

Here you could find out every other article related to cooking. In this one, I may not expound on suppers, but approximately paintings withinside the kitchen. You want to keep in mind that arranging is 1/2 of of the achievement (in cooking, but in severa components of our life), so previous to cooking you want to get prepared and plan the whole thing cautiously. In this text, I would possibly need to expound on easy plans for right paintings withinside the kitchen.

Above all else, you could enhance your cooking through utilising simply easy plans. You may not want to do a ton of factors and all matters considered, you may not want to easy a tremendous deal. There are masses of plans for a few dishes, so every person can find out and prepare dinner dinner some thing for himself/herself.

The following tremendous opportunity to enhance your kitchen paintings is planning. Before you start cooking, you want to layout the whole thing cautiously. You must take a look at fixings and also you want to take all apparatuses with a purpose to be vital to put together your feast. There is a standard, it says which you must area the principle gadgets inside your reach.

It is a surely agreeable desire which could spare a tremendous deal of time this is giant withinside the kitchen. Presently I will focus on every other a part of the easy components for right paintings withinside the kitchen.

Presently I will compose a pair of factors approximately the kitchen space. It's vital to have tremendous mild on this spot because you want to understand what you're doing (mainly whilst you are slicing some thing).

Recall that dividers and flooring for your kitchen must be something however tough to easy. You need to likewise don't forget tremendous air flow withinside the kitchen.

It's perfect seeing that it improves your paintings and it is beneficial to your wellbeing. You can likewise make use of a few different equipment which could enhance your paintings, for example, kitchen robots and so forth As I would really like to assume it is a easy components for respectable paintings withinside the kitchen.

That is all I had to write on this component approximately the great and easy plans for right paintings withinside the kitchen. Recollect my advice and I'm sure that your cooking may be improved. You may not have any problems and making ready supper (or every other feast) may be a pleasure for you.

I agree with you found perusing this text intriguing. I'm placing forth a valiant attempt and withinside the following article, I will deliver greater records approximately easy plans for right paintings withinside the kitchen. I will compose this text, later on, so please stand through with persistence.

Healthy Easy Recipes And Ways

For sure individuals, the errand of getting ready a natively built supper is brimming with ordinary complexities. The manner to less expensive meals and eliminate suppers seems to in shape flawlessly into occupied methods of lifestyles and livid own circle of relatives lifestyles, paintings and social timetables, in lots of instances swallowed down with little concept regarding what the fixings certainly are, the vicinity in which they got here from, and the way they had been advanced and cooked. I will display you later an outstanding asset for plans, simply as treasured markdown cookbooks and well being and well-being tips.

Solid Easy Recipes

Preparing a dinner party does not want to be muddled.

The usage of spices continuously will hoist your cooking to a delectable new level. Try now no longer to assume you want to shuffle numerous pots and field simultaneously, with the aid of using the equal token. There are a whole lot of outstanding plans that simply require one pot. It's what you install that pot that has the effect.

Step with the aid of using step commands to Prepare Healthy Meals

Another tip in the direction of stable easy plans is to heat up for your cooler. Rather than viewing a inconsiderate TV drama, make investments a few electricity to create a supper or that may be flown withinside the cooler and pulled out for a second supper whilst time is short. You'll be surprised how high quality this may make to your suppers.

Diagram your culinary direction with care and do not allow your nutritional manner get diverted media exposure and captivating commercials. Despite the reality that fee is significant, it's miles in addition vital to peruse meals marks and talent to decipher them.

Fixing names are often little to debilitate your examination, so set apart the attempt to understand what to look for.

Keep farfar from High Salt and Sugar Content

Specialists coach to live away with appreciate to excessive sodium and sugar content, hurtful or substance additives, and counterfeit delivered substances. We are altogether getting drastically greater privy to what is in our meals, and makers are controlled and devoted to show what is of their items.

Keep Your Family Healthy

Solid easy plans repay in preserving you and your own circle of relatives unit sound and assist in constructing your safety from pain and infection. You and your family can cheer that the onions had been sautéed with out spread, the serving of blended veggies dressing isn't always made with low first-rate oil, the soup tastes delectable with each unmarried ordinary fixing, the beans are delicious, the beef is lean and sans fat, the rice is nutritious, the goods of the soil are obviously advanced, and the pastry is brimming with transgression loose goodness.

SARA

JACKLINE